A MISCELLANY

Compiled by Julia Skinner

With particular reference to the work of Martin Andrew

THE FRANCIS FRITH COLLECTION

www.francisfrith.com

First published in the United Kingdom in 2006 by The Francis Frith Collection®

This edition published exclusively for Oakridge Books & Gifts in 2010 ISBN 978-1-84589-551-8
Oakridge, Greenstalls Park, Costello Hill, Ilchester, Somerset BA22 8LB. Tel: 08453 893293

British Library Cataloguing in Publication Data

Did You Know? Aylesbury - A Miscellany
Compiled by Julia Skinner
With particular reference to the work of Martin Andrew

The Francis Frith Collection
Frith's Barn, Teffont,
Salisbury, Wiltshire SP3 5QP
Tel: +44 (0) 1722 716 376
Email: info@francisfrith.co.uk
www.francisfrith.com

Printed and bound in England

Front Cover: **AYLESBURY, THE CANAL 1897** 39642p

The colour-tinting is for illustrative purposes only, and is not intended to be historically accurate

AS WITH ANY HISTORICAL DATABASE, THE FRANCIS FRITH ARCHIVE IS CONSTANTLY BEING CORRECTED AND IMPROVED, AND THE PUBLISHERS WOULD WELCOME INFORMATION ON OMISSIONS OR INACCURACIES

CONTENTS

INTRODUCTION

Aylesbury is situated on a hill that would have provided a natural defensive position in earlier times; evidence of Iron Age settlement has been found which has led archaeologists to speculate that there may perhaps have been an Iron Age hillfort here. Roman finds are more sparse, and do not suggest a Roman settlement on the hill, despite the fact that the road known to the Anglo-Saxons as Akeman Street - which ran from Verulamium (St Albans) to Corinium (Cirencester) - passed along the northern slopes of Aylesbury's hill. Aylesbury was an established town in the Anglo-Saxon period, and the Domesday Book of 1086 refers to market tolls in Aylesbury with a value of £10. The Middle Ages saw Aylesbury grow into a prosperous market town with two market places. The town was a market centre for a large hinterland, with its livestock and crops supplying the ever-growing London market. There was apparently a royal castle somewhere in Aylesbury at one time, but its only trace is in the name of Castle Street.

Aylesbury effectively took over from a declining Buckingham as the county town of Buckinghamshire in Henry VIII's reign, when the summer assize courts transferred here, to the geographical centre of the county; by the 17th century, the circuit judges heard county cases only in Aylesbury.

This ancient hill town prospered in the 18th century, deriving much of its wealth from agriculture in the improved rich soils of the Vale of Aylesbury and success in enterprises such as corn growing and duck rearing; there was also a local lace-making industry. Aylesbury has expanded considerably in the last 150 years: in the late 19th century, speculators drained marshy ground and built housing estates beyond the old town centre, such as Manor Park, Albion Street off the High Street and Queens Park on the other side of the canal, and the housing of Victoria Park on the north side of the Tring Road. More growth came after the First World War, and again after the Second World War when housing was built to absorb some of the London overspill. Housing, industrial and commercial development has continued ever since, and further growth is planned for the future.

Aylesbury is now a busy modern town at the junction of six main roads, but its centre recalls more leisurely days. Narrow Tudor alleys run between four squares - St Mary's, Market, Temple and Kingsbury. The historic Georgian core of the town escaped redevelopment in the 1960s and deserves exploration, especially since traffic has largely been removed from Market Square.

The story of Aylesbury is full of fascinating characters and events, of which this book can only provide a brief glimpse.

HIGH STREET 1897 39625

BUCKINGHAMSHIRE DIALECT WORDS AND PHRASES

'Bucks Bread and Beef' used to be a saying reflecting the fact that Buckinghamshire supplied a good deal of both butter and cattle for the London market.

'Dimpsey' - dusk, twilight.

'Oddy doddies' - snails.

'Dabster' - proficient, as in 'He's a dabster at it'.

'Abroadyday' - out of doors, in the open air.

'Devil's darning needle' - a dragon fly.

'Afeard' - afraid.

'Hurrocky' - hurried, hasty.

'Airywig' - an earwig.

'Hedgepig' - a hedgehog.

'Maggled' - flushed with heat, feverish, flustered.

'Mommered' - dazed or confused.

HAUNTED AYLESBURY

The ancient King's Head Inn in Aylesbury is supposed to be haunted by several ghosts. One of the best known is the Grey Lady who is said to stand in the Great Hall, warming herself by the fire. Another ghost, sightings of which have been reported in the corridor by the red staircase, is believed to be that of a maid who died there in an accident c1900.

The Saracen's Head pub is believed to be haunted by the ghost of a local man called George, who moves tables and chairs around at night, accompanied by mysterious banging sounds.

There have been reports of a ghost at Creslow Manor near Aylesbury. The sound of light footsteps running down corridors has been heard, accompanied by rustling, as of a silk dress.

Hartwell House Hotel is said to be haunted by the ghost of a former owner, called Lee, who wanders around the library and garden.

A few miles outside Aylesbury, the junction of the A418 and a lane leading to Haddenham is said to be haunted by the ghost of a man called Noble Eddon, who was murdered in the early 19th century by two local men called Tylor and Sewell. Noble had witnessed the two men stealing sheep, and they killed him to keep him quiet. It is said that the ghost is bleeding from a chest wound, and that anyone who sees the apparition will be cursed with a run of bad luck.

AYLESBURY MISCELLANY

Aylesbury appears for the first time in written history under its Saxon name of Aeglesburge. The 'Anglo-Saxon Chronicle' records under AD571 that 'Cuthla fought against the Britons at Biedcanford and captured four villages, Limbury, Aylesbury (Aeglesburge), Benson and Eynsham', and in a will of about AD970, Aylesbury was bequeathed to King Edgar by Aelfheah, Ealdorman of Hampshire.

According to tradition, an Anglo-Saxon noblewoman called Edith was 'lady' of the town of Aylesbury in the 7th century. Edith was possibly the Christian princess daughter (or grand-daughter) of King Penda of Mercia and the aunt of St Osyth. St Osyth is said to have been born at Quarrendon in Buckinghamshire, and to have been brought up at Aylesbury by her aunt Edith; her remains are believed to have been interred in St Mary's Church in Aylesbury for some time after her martyrdom at the hands of Danish marauders at Chich in Essex in AD653. St Osyth's burial place at Aylesbury became a place of pilgrimage, but some sources say that her remains were removed to a church at Chich six years later, and others that they were removed by Papal decree in 1500 and buried in secret elsewhere. Whatever the truth, the fact remains that a grant of 1239 mentions the 'old fair on the feast of St Osyth in the Summer' (3 June) in Aylesbury, which points to some connection between Aylesbury and the saint. The 17th-century antiquary John Aubrey recorded an old custom associated with St Osyth: 'In those days, when they went to bed they did rake up the fire, and make a X on the ashes, and pray to God and St Sythe (that is St Osyth) to deliver them from fire, and from water, and from all misadventure'.

THE WAR MEMORIAL AND THE JOHN HAMPDEN STATUE c1955 A84026

ST MARY'S CHURCH 1927 79560

Aylesbury's parish church of St Mary (see photograph 79560, above) has long been thought to be the successor of an Anglo-Saxon minster church. Minster churches are often cruciform, ie with a crossing tower and transepts. This theory received some support when excavations within the nave of the church in 1978 uncovered clear evidence of a late Anglo-Saxon church. The present church is mostly 13th-century, but it was heavily restored by Sir George Gilbert Scott between 1849 and 1869.

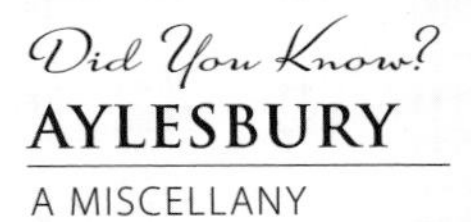

There was a mint in the Anglo-Saxon town of Aylesbury: silver pennies produced by eight moniers have been found. Coins were issued from here in the 10th century during the reigns of Ethelred 'the Unready', (AD978–1016), Canute (1016–35), and Edward the Confessor (1042–66), the names of the moniers respectively being Aelfgar, Aelfwi, and Wulfred.

All the houses on the left of photograph 70559 of Church Street (below) have been bought by the Thomas Hickman Charity in recent years, and refurbished. Thomas Hickman, born in 1695, founded a charity which built almshouses; it is still an active charity in Aylesbury, which buys and refurbishes houses and cottages in the old town for rent.

CHURCH STREET 1921 70559

KINGSBURY SQUARE 1921 70556

The Red Lion on the left of this photograph is now the Hobgoblin. The drinking fountain seen in the photograph was installed in 1914, but was removed in 1929 when a bus station was erected in Kingsbury Square; the fountain was later installed in The Vale park. Beyond the fountain in the photograph is a tank from the First World War, which was parked in the square in 1920; when the tank was being dismantled in 1929, it exploded - it must have contained some live ammunition all through the time that it was sitting in the square!

MARKET SQUARE 1901 47462

A livestock sale is under way in photograph 47462, above, with the auctioneer's tent behind the clock tower. On the left the pipe-smoker sits on his hurdle wagon waiting to collect the livestock pens after the sale has finished. The clock tower was erected in 1876 on the approximate site of the old market house, which was pulled down in 1866 to enlarge the market place. The lion drowsing on its plinth is one of a pair of French cast-iron statues, a gift from Ferdinand, Baron Rothschild of Waddesdon Manor in 1887.

The first recorded tornado in the United Kingdom struck the Vale of Aylesbury on Sunday, 21 May 1950. It started in Wendover and moved on to Halton. The force of the tornado was such that at Halton a few aircraft were lifted off the aerodrome, and in Aston Clinton a number of cattle sheds were blown up by the wind to hang from trees.

Several street names in Aylesbury have been changed over the years: High Street was originally called New Road, and Cambridge Street, which misleadingly does not head for Cambridge, was formerly Bakers Lane.

Photograph 70558 (below) shows the view past the Bell Hotel down Walton Street in 1921 - a scene now much changed. At the right of the photograph the jewellers, the Greyhound on the east side of Market Square, and the buildings beyond on the right-hand side of Walton Street are part of what was demolished in the early 1960s for the Friars Square shopping centre and the new County Offices; the latter is a twelve-storey tower block, visible for miles around and much-disliked, nicknamed 'Fred's Folly' after Fred Pooley, the County Architect at the time of its construction.

WALTON STREET 1921 70558

The King's Head, one of Aylesbury's architectural treasures, is tucked away off the Market Square. It was given by the Rothschilds to the National Trust in 1926, and underwent major and scholarly restoration in the 1990s. Photograph 47466, opposite, shows the 15th-century Great Hall window, ten lights wide with arched upper lights. Some original glass still survives, a remarkable and rare survival amid the bustle of an inn through over five and a half centuries, including armorial glass with the coat of arms of Henry VI and Margaret of Anjou, which dates from 1456: the king and his wife are believed to have stayed at the inn while on a tour of the country after their marriage.

During the Civil War, Aylesbury was stoutly pro-Parliamentarian (there is a statue of John Hampden, one of the Parliamentary leaders who lived nearby at Prestwood Common, in the Market Square). At the outbreak of the war the town was garrisoned for Parliament, and volunteers from London set up a pulpit in the market place and plundered the houses of Papists. The town was subject to several attacks from Charles I's headquarters in Oxford, some led by the dashing cavalry leader Prince Rupert, the king's nephew, and there are Civil War siege earthworks at Quarrendon.

In St Mary's Church is an alabaster monument which commemorates the wife and three children of Sir Henry Lee, an ancestor of the American Civil War general Robert E Lee. An inscription on the monument asks for crimson flowers to be placed on Lady Lee's tomb, and the request has been honoured ever since her death in 1584.

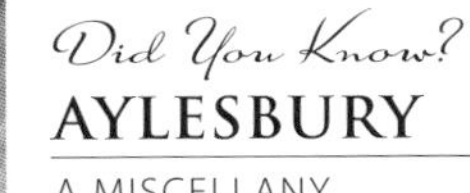

THE KING'S HEAD HOTEL, THE ANCIENT WINDOW 1901 47466

COUNTY HALL 1897 39626

The south side of the Market Square is dominated in photograph 39626 (above) by the very fine Georgian former County Hall, built for the county assizes. It was a long time a-building, taking from 1722 until 1737. The central arched window once had a balcony outside, which was the public scaffold from which criminals were hanged. After a disastrous fire in 1970 the interior of the courts was lovingly recreated, accurate in every detail down to the crested chamber pot behind the judge's seat. This building now houses the Crown Court, and an uncompromisingly modern building close by is now County Hall.

Behind Kingsbury is St Mary's Square, which is in fact the churchyard of the medieval parish church and a green oasis in the town. Photograph A84022, below, shows the view looking north past the 1840s Old Parish School, which is now part of the County Museum - the second gable is a 1907 replica. Beyond are cottages which were at one time the parish poorhouse, where the deserving poor made lace and baked bread.

In 1832 the whole of England was hit by an epidemic of cholera, a deadly intestinal infection caused by eating or drinking contaminated food or water. Aylesbury was struck so hard by the disease that it is said that travellers made a detour to avoid the town. The Royal Buckinghamshire Hospital was founded at this time, in response to the cholera outbreak.

ST MARY'S SQUARE c1955 A84022

At the bottom end of the High Street is The Vale, a park formally opened in 1937 in fields between the now vanished London and North Western Railway station, which was demolished in 1960, and the gas works, also now gone. Now a smart covered

THE VALE PARK c1950 A84007

swimming pool replaces the old open-air Vale Pool, but the park is relatively little changed from the view shown in A84007, below. The drinking fountain was originally installed in 1914 in Kingsbury, but was moved here after 1929.

MARKET SQUARE c1955 A84032

The Civil War battle of Aylesbury was fought at Holman's Bridge, over the young River Thame on the Buckingham road a mile north of the town, on 1 November 1642. According to Parliamentary reports, Prince Rupert marched his forces into Aylesbury on his way to London after the battle of Edgehill. Hearing of this, 1,500 men under the Parliamentarian Sir William Balfour came to the aid of the townspeople. Prince Rupert met Balfour's forces outside the town at Holman's Bridge, from where his forces were driven away by the Parliamentarians, aided by a number of Aylesbury men who attacked their unwelcome guests from the rear, forcing the Royalists to retire towards Oxford.

At the left of photograph 39626 on page 16 is the Jacobean-style Corn Exchange of 1865. This was a very important building in its day, where farmers and grain merchants bartered for, and fixed, the price of grain. In a rural community, where most people were directly or indirectly involved with agriculture, this was where decisions and commerce took place that affected the economy of the whole district. The corn exchange of most large country towns was usually a grand imposing building which doubled as a venue for public entertainments, such as concerts and plays, although the corn exchange in Aylesbury is less grand than some of its contemporaries. The building was erected by a consortium of local businessmen who called themselves the Aylesbury Market Company. They purchased and demolished the old White Hart Inn, and replaced it with a new cattle market and the Corn Exchange. An agricultural depression from the 1870s resulted in farming becoming less profitable; the Corn Exchange never realised the profits its builders had hoped for, and the building was sold in 1901 to the Urban District Council for use as a town hall.

Probably the original market place, Kingsbury Square was laid out in the Middle Ages and has several good old buildings including the 16th-century The Rookwood (now the Lobster Pot). The houses on the left of photograph 47464, opposite, which were shops in 1901 but still with their front gardens, were replaced in the 1960s by offices over a shop. Beyond them, the tall building is the Victoria Working Men's Club, built in 1887 to commemorate Queen Victoria's Golden Jubilee and funded by Baron Rothschild of Waddesdon. The square is actually triangular, and until it was paved was often knee-deep in mud.

A few weeks after Aylesbury people had helped to drive away Royalist forces at the battle of Aylesbury on 1 November 1642, they took up arms a second time to defend their homes and property when some Royalist cavalry quartered themselves in the town. These unwelcome visitors made themselves highly unpopular, plundering and wrecking houses, until the townsmen and local villagers armed themselves with pikes and muskets and drove them from the market place, where they had made a stand.

Photograph 70564, opposite, shows a pair of loaded working boats on the Aylesbury Arm near Broughton on the edge of town. The wooden stumps seen in the bottom left corner of the photograph are known as strapping posts, and were used to tie up boats.

KINGSBURY SQUARE 1901 47464

THE AYLESBURY ARM, THE GRAND UNION CANAL 1921 70564

MARKET SQUARE 1921 70551

At the left of photograph 70551 (above) of the Market Square is the 1911 statue of John Hampden, the great Parliamentary leader of the 1630s and the English Civil War. It was moved 50ft east in 1988, under the careful watch of Civil War re-enactors. It now stands nearer the statue of the Victorian Tory Prime Minister Benjamin Disraeli, which was erected in 1914 - they seem to be carefully avoiding each other's eyes.

Photograph 70551 above shows a livestock sale in the Market Square in 1921, the sheep penned and the cattle tied to improvised rails. The last livestock market in the square took place a few years later, in 1927.

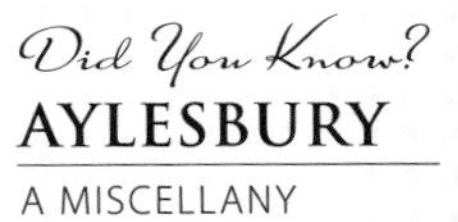

A few miles outside Aylesbury at the summit of Lodge Hill is the French chateau-style Waddesdon Manor. It was built by the French architect Hippolyte Alexandre Gabriel Walter Destailleur for Baron Ferdinand de Rothschild, who had bought the estate in 1872. Lodge Hill was then a bare hill, but the Baron imported vast numbers of mature trees to give it its present wooded character; teams of horses toiled from far and wide to haul the trees to their destination. The hilltop was levelled to accommodate the house, its parterres and approaches. The design draws on a number of French chateaux; it has a wonderfully complex roofscape, while inside is a spectacular collection of panelling, chimneypieces, boiseries and fittings, salvaged from French mansions, as well as priceless collections of porcelain and antiques. Waddesdon Manor is now an immensely popular attraction owned by the National Trust.

WADDESDON, THE MANOR, THE SOUTH FRONT 1897 39653

The splendidly ornate Hazell, Watson and Viney Printing Works and chimney, seen in photograph 39638, opposite, were an important part of Aylesbury's industrial life from their opening in 1878 to their demolition in the 1980s. By the late 19th century this printing and bookbinding company and the Nestlé works were the two main employers in Aylesbury - it has been estimated that half the working population of the town worked for these two companies. The site of the Hazell, Watson and Viney Printing Works has now been redeveloped for housing.

The railway arrived in Aylesbury in 1839 as a branch line from the London and North West Railway. Its station was originally near the junction of Station and Railway Streets, and was then rebuilt in 1889 fronting onto the High Street near the Exchange Street station. This line was lifted and the station demolished in 1960; Aylesbury's second station is now the town's only one. This opened as a branch from the Great Western Railway's Princes Risborough station in 1863, which was extended to Verney Junction in 1868. This station also served the Metropolitan Railway, which reached Aylesbury in 1892 - they rebuilt the station at the same time. The Metropolitan abandoned Aylesbury, only serving Buckinghamshire as far out as Amersham, and the line was taken over by the Great Central for its route to Nottingham and Sheffield. Nowadays Aylesbury is the terminus of the Chiltern Railway from Marylebone, and only freight traffic goes beyond the town.

Aylesbury has recently been awarded £1 million in funding to become one of six Cycling Demonstration towns in England. Under this scheme, Buckinghamshire County Council hopes to promote the use of cycling amongst the general public, and undertakes to provide facilities around the town for cyclists such as bike lockers and bike stands, as well as Tiger and Toucan road crossings.

THE HAZELL, WATSON AND VINEY PRINTING WORKS 1897 39638

THE MILK FACTORY 1897 39640

AYLESBURY DUCKS c1955 A84044

The name of Aylesbury is known to many people because of the distinctive heavy breed of duck which was developed in the 18th century for the London meat market. The ducks were driven on foot (but later transported in railway carriages) to Smithfield and other markets. They were bred in Aylesbury and the surrounding villages, including Walton and Haddenham, whose ponds were of great use, and at Weston Turville, which alone sent 25,000 ducklings a year to London in the 1890s. The true Aylesbury duck is now virtually extinct - the last known flock was at Chesham in the 1980s.

Aylesbury still has a number of important early buildings in the town: there are timber-framed buildings in the island between Kingsbury and Buckingham Street, and, apart from the 13th-century parish church, there are pre-1600 buildings such as a cruck house in Castle Street, the Lobster Pot (ex-The Rookwood) and the Hobgoblin (ex-Red Lion) in Kingsbury, and No 2 Church Street, which is datable to around 1546.

The font in St Mary's Church in the town is circular and carved with stiff-leaved foliage round the rim and base. The style is so distinctive that it has given its name to a type: 'Aylesbury' fonts resemble gold chalices with fluted sides set on ornate carved bases. Another fine example of a 12th-century Norman stone 'Aylesbury' font can be seen in the church at Great Kimble, a few miles south of the town.

Parson's Fee leads uphill from Castle Street towards the church and then St Osyths, a good brick house of about 1700, its facade now painted. Beyond it are the grounds of The Prebendal, behind high brick walls. From 1757 to 1764 this was the home of John Wilkes, the satirist and radical MP who represented Aylesbury for seven years. He was twice expelled from the House of Commons for his attacks on George III and his government.

PARSON'S FEE c1965 A84097

At the junction of Buckingham and Bicester Roads is the Royal Buckinghamshire Hospital. David Brandon rebuilt the hospital between 1859-62 in a similar style to the earlier one, a Georgian country house with wings added in 1832. He was advised by Florence Nightingale herself, and it was the first post-Crimean War hospital where her precepts about hospital design were put into practice.

Lace-making was once an important industry in Aylesbury and there are some fine examples of Buckinghamshire lace to be seen in the Buckinghamshire County Museum. Queen Victoria was once quoted as preferring 'Bucks lace' for her pillows. Buckinghamshire lace became very sought after, but was mainly made by poor women and children; pauper children in poorhouses were often taught to make lace in Lace Schools in the 17th century, which would provide them with a means of making a living. Bucks Point - Buckinghamshire lace - was a very 'lacy' style, with a characteristic hexagon 'ground' of fine white cotton or silk with a white 'gimp' (heavier) thread worked through for emphasis. Buckinghamshire lace was a bobbin lace, which is also known as bone lace, as the bobbins were often made from bone. Lace-making was not a healthy job; the lace-makers often had poor eyesight in later life, and many of them developed a stoop, from bending over their work from a young age. In the second half of the 19th century the cottage industry of lace-making was unable to compete with machine-made lace, and died out.

The edible, or squirrel-tailed, dormouse was introduced into Tring Park in 1902, and is now breeding in the countryside around Aylesbury. These nocturnal animals are famous in history as being a favourite delicacy of Roman cuisine, usually stuffed, but are not eaten today. They live in deciduous woodland, and sometimes find their way into houses to hibernate.

THE BUCKS COUNTY INFIRMARY 1897 39629

HIGH STREET c1955 A84055

THE CANAL AND THE HILLS & PARTRIDGES LOCK 1921 39643

First authorised in the 1790s, the Aylesbury Arm running from the Grand Junction Canal (later the Grand Union Canal) at Marsworth across the Vale of Aylesbury finally opened in 1815. Coal was one of the main early imports. Photograph 39643, above, shows a view of the canal, looking towards the town past Lock No 16, Hills & Partridges Lock, to the original brick canal bridge, rebuilt in 1900. This lock was the last before the canal boats reached the canal basin at Walton Street, where a cargo crane is preserved.

Coal wharves at the canal basin by Walton Street were soon joined by factories along the canal. One that arrived in 1870 to take advantage both of the canal and the milk from the Vale of Aylesbury dairy herds was the Anglo-Swiss Condensed Milk Company, seen in photograph 39640 on page 27. It later became the Nestle's factory, a major employer in the town.

A Franciscan friary was established in Aylesbury c1386 by James Butler, Earl of Ormonde, who was lord of the manor at that time. The former friarage is now 14 Bourbon Street; although it has been re-fronted several times, it is one of the oldest buildings in Aylesbury, and part of its original foundations can be seen at the side, in Friarage Passage. The friary was surrendered to the Crown at Henry VIII's Dissolution, in October 1538, and the building was bought by the lord of the manor, Sir John Baldwin, in April 1541. The building is now used as offices by a long-established firm of solicitors.

Foundations and stonework from Aylesbury's medieval Franciscan friary have been found in the grounds of a house in the town, and also pieces of a 15th-century window. In the County Museum in the town are some stone fragments which were probably part of a tomb, which represent figures of two weeping women.

KINGSBURY c1960 A84112

CAMBRIDGE STREET c1955 A84028

In the early 18th century the local Aylesbury worthies decided to build a grand and magnificent new County Hall. Plans were submitted by two architects, a Mr Brandon and a Mr Thomas Harris. The final decision on which plan to use was to be made by no less than the famous architect John Vanbrugh. This was a system that was used quite often by civic bodies commissioning architecture all over the country when money was tight: for a fraction of the price of employing a great architect, a famous name would be forever associated with the building if he could be persuaded to judge a competition to choose the best design. This is what happened at Aylesbury, where Vanbrugh's name is remembered in connection with the County Hall while the local architect who designed it, Thomas Harris, is almost forgotten.

The gaol for the county of Buckinghamshire and the forest of Bernwood was at Aylesbury from at least 1180. It was repaired c1182 under the supervision of 'David de Aylesbury' and 'Herbert de Bierton'. Records show that in 1276 the gaoler was allowing women to escape for the sum of 1 shilling a head. In spite of repairs executed in the early 14th century the prison was still insecure in 1340, when felons escaped in considerable numbers.

During the Second World War a hospital was set up at Stoke Mandeville, just outside Aylesbury, under the wartime Emergency Medical Services arrangements. In 1944 a National Spinal Injuries Centre was set up at the hospital by Dr Ludwig Guttman, and Stoke Mandeville Hospital is now internationally renowned for its specialist expertise in the treatment and rehabilitation of patients with such injuries. The Stoke Mandeville stadium was the venue for the first paraplegic games in 1954, which helped to promote and establish paralympic sport.

The town was the focus of international attention in the 1960s when the culprits responsible for the Great Train Robbery were tried at Aylesbury. This notorious robbery took place at Bridego Bridge, a railway bridge between the villages of Cheddington and Linslade, about six miles from Aylesbury, on 8 August 1963. The raiders ambushed the Royal Mail train from Scotland to Euston, and got away with £2.5 million in old bank notes, after seriously injuring the train driver.

HIGH STREET 1921 70557

A few miles to the south-east of Aylesbury is Chequers, the country residence of the Prime Minister of the United Kingdom. The house was used as a hospital during the First World War, and then as a convalescent home. After the war the house was restored to the owners, Lord and Lady Lee of Farnham. The Lees were childless, and decided to offer their house to the nation as a country retreat for the serving Prime Minister. They realised that up until that date most prime ministers had come from the aristocracy and already had their own country houses to use, but that a new era was dawning in which prime ministers were being drawn from different social backgrounds and might not privately own a country house suitable for such purposes as entertaining foreign heads of state. A commemorative window in the long gallery of the house was commissioned by Lord and Lady Lee which bears the inscription: 'This house of peace and ancient memories was given to England as a thank-offering for her deliverance in the great war of 1914-1918 as a place of rest and recreation for her Prime Ministers for ever.'

The Buckinghamshire County Museum is partly housed in Ceely House in Church Street; its Georgian front conceals a superb timber frame of c1472 which was originally built as the Brotherhood House of the Fraternity of the Virgin Mary, a religious organisation connected with St Mary's Church. The building was used as a ceremonial space for meetings and as offices for the Fraternity. It was not used as a habitation, but the upstairs room may have been lodgings for a priest, although it could only be reached by an outside staircase. There is a wall painting on display which dates from the late 15th century.

THE HAZELL, WATSON AND VINEY PRINTING WORKS 1897 39639

MARKET SQUARE 1901 47461

AYLESBURY CHILDREN 1897 39627x

The County Gaol in Aylesbury was designed by a Major J Jebb in 1845. The original design was in line with Victorian ideas about crime and punishment, in which prisoners were kept in complete solitary confinement for the entire duration of their sentence. 250 men ate, slept and washed alone and in silence, leaving their individual cells only to worship at the prison chapel. This chapel (described by Pevsner as 'elegantly built') had 247 seats, but they were designed so the convicts could not see each other during the service. The prison still stands, the main facade largely unchanged, and remains a prison, although the inmates are kept in considerably more enlightened conditions nowadays.

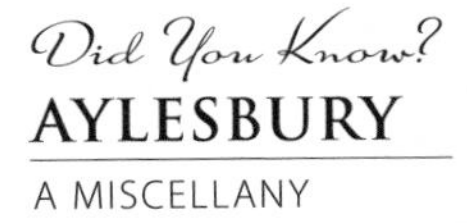

The popular children's author Roald Dahl lived for many years until his death in 1990 in the Buckinghamshire village of Great Missenden. He is commemorated in Aylesbury by the award-winning Roald Dahl Children's Gallery at the Buckinghamshire County Museum in Church Street. This museum uses characters and themes from Roald Dahl's books to stimulate and develop children's interest in science, history and literature; the work of the museum is enhanced by the graphics which were provided by Quentin Blake, whose work was used for cover designs and illustrations for many of the books.

MARKET SQUARE c1955 A84005

Chequers, the country residence of the Prime Minister, was originally a Tudor house, but has been remodelled and extended several times over the centuries. It is known that one John Hawtrey restored and enlarged the house in 1565, and this same John Hawtrey was responsible for guarding a royal prisoner in the house, Lady Mary Grey, the sister of the tragic 'Nine Days Queen', Lady Jane Grey, who was executed in 1553. Lady Mary Grey, who was described as 'four foot tall and hunchbacked', was the great grand-daughter of Henry VII and a distant cousin of Elizabeth I. She had dared to marry a royal gatekeeper, Thomas Keyes, without her family's consent, and was banished from court by Queen Elizabeth, who ordered her to be kept confined to ensure 'there were no little bastards' who might present a challenge to her throne. Mary lived at Chequers for two years, from 1565 to 1567, and the room where she slept is still kept much as it was during her enforced visit to the house. She was released after her husband died in 1572 and permitted to attend court again, and died childless at the age of 33.

The poor state of the roads in earlier days is well illustrated by a sad tale from 1499 of a glover who set out on a journey in the early hours of the morning from Leighton Buzzard to Aylesbury market. As he rode along in the dark on a horse laden with panniers of gloves, both horse and rider fell into a pit in the road. The pit had been dug earlier by servants of a local miller who had needed clay to repair his mill; they left a hole in the road 10ft wide and 8ft deep, which soon filled with water from the winter rains. The unfortunate glover and his horse were both drowned. The miller was taken to court over this incident, but when he explained to the court that the road was the only place he could get the heavy clay he needed, it was judged that his action was quite reasonable and he was released without punishment.

SPORTING AYLESBURY

Aylesbury United FC has a long history, going back to 1897. Over that time the team seems to have always played in its distinctive green and white stripes.

In 1988 Aylesbury United became the only non-League team to play against the full England team. Football greats like Gary Lineker and Peter Beardsley turned out at United's Buckingham Road Stadium in a warm up match for the European championships.

Surely one of Aylesbury's most notable sporting characters is Cliff Hercules. He was the most prolific Aylesbury United player of all time, scoring 301 goals in 669 games. He was a member of the team that played against England in 1988.

Aylesbury Hockey Club has a long and proud history. Founded in 1948, its playing highlights include two South of England playoffs. Two of its finest players were Harry Cahill, Great Britain's most capped international goalkeeper, and Great Britain's centre forward Brian Disbury.

In recent times Aylesbury has been very productive in the realm of sporting talent. Recent successful sportsmen include these Aylesbury natives: Jon Lewis, Gloucester and England cricketer; Samuel Ricketts, Swansea city footballer; Emerson Boyce, Crystal Palace footballer; and Andrew Triggs-Hodge, winner of a World Cup rowing gold medal in 2005.

QUIZ QUESTIONS

Answers on page 48.

1. What happened for the last time in Aylesbury in 1845?
2. In Market Square is a statue of John Hampden (1594-1643), who was mortally wounded during the Civil War in a fight with Royalist troops at Chalgrove Field in 1643. John Hampden was famous for his opposition to Charles I over the matter of Ship Money - what was this?
3. How did Parson's Fee get its name?
4. Who stands between two lions in Market Square?
5. Which of Henry VIII's six wives had links with Aylesbury?
6. Why is Euclid Neale a famous name connected with Aylesbury?
7. One of the prominent buildings in Aylesbury is the 'Blue Leanie' office block, which is home to Halifax Bank of Scotland (HBOS). Why was it considered to be a dangerous building when it was first built?
8. What is the connection between Oliver Cromwell and Chequers, the country residence of the Prime Minister, a few miles south-east of Aylesbury?
9. A very special car has the Aylesbury registration plate BH 9723 - what is this car, and where can you see it?
10. Which monarch kept chickens on the roof of Hartwell House, near Aylesbury?

THE BELL HOTEL 1921 70563

RECIPE

DUCK WITH PORT AND REDCURRANT SAUCE

Ingredients
4 duck portions
Grated rind and juice of 1 lemon
Grated rind and juice of 1 orange
4 tablespoons redcurrant jelly
4 tablespoons port
1 tablespoon brandy
A pinch of ground mace or ginger
Salt and pepper

Preheat the oven to 190 degrees C/375 degrees F/ Gas Mark 5. Place a rack in a roasting tin. Prick the duck portions all over with a fork, and sprinkle with salt and pepper. Place the duck portions on the rack in the roasting tin and cook in the oven for 45-50 minutes, until the skin is crisp and the juices run clear.

Simmer the lemon and orange juices and rinds together in a saucepan for 5 minutes. Stir in the redcurrant jelly until melted, then stir in the port. Bring to the boil, and add the mace or ginger and seasoning to taste.

Transfer the duck to a serving plate and keep warm. Pour off the fat from the roasting tin, leaving the cooking juices. With the tin over a low heat, stir in the brandy, dislodging the sediment, and bring to the boil. Stir in the port and redcurrant mixture to make the sauce, and serve with the duck.

ST MARY'S CHURCH, THE CHANCEL 1897 39636

MARKET SQUARE 1901 47463

RECIPE

AYLESBURY CHERRY BUMPERS

Ingredients
450g/1lb black cherries
75g/3oz sugar
225g/8oz shortcrust pastry

Stone the cherries and sprinkle them with sugar. Roll out the pastry and cut into 10cm (4 inch) rounds. Heap the centre of each pastry round with cherries. Damp the edges of the pastry and fold one half of each round over the filling to make a pasty shape, and seal the edges by pinching them together with your fingers. Bake at 200 degrees C/400 degrees F/Gas Mark 6 for about 25 minutes. Dredge with sugar and cool on a wire rack.

QUIZ ANSWERS

1. The last public execution in Aylesbury took place from the scaffold at the County Hall in 1845. The 'Quaker poisoner' John Tawall was hanged there, having been apprehended in London from a description telegraphed from Slough station to Paddington - an early and sensational use of the new medium.

2. Ship Money was a form of tax, or contribution, which was levied upon the maritime counties and ports of England in times of national emergency for the maintenance of ships for the country's defence. This form of taxation was extended to include all of England by Charles I in 1635 to increase his income, in the period just before the Civil War when he had fallen out with Parliament. The legality of the tax was challenged by Aylesbury's John Hampden, and a massive campaign of tax refusal ensued.

3. In the Middle Ages a number of new smaller landholdings were created by royal grant, which were often known as 'fees'. Aylesbury had several 'fees' which included the Castle Fee (which was held by the principal lord of the manor of Aylesbury, who also held the Lord's Fee); the Otterer's Fee (which was granted to Roger Foll, the king's otter hunter in 1179) and Church Fee (or Parson's Fee), which was endowed to the Church. From the Norman Conquest until 1845 the parish of Aylesbury belonged to the Bishop of Lincoln, and its vicars were appointed by a prebendary, or honorary canon, of Lincoln Cathedral. The road at the top of Church Street is called Parson's Fee because the land around it once belonged to the Prebendal Farm.

4. Between the lions in Market Square is a statue of Major-General Charles Compton, 3rd Baron Chesham, the commander of the Bucks Militia, who fought in South Africa during the Boer War (see photograph A84032 on page 20).

5. His second wife, Anne Boleyn. Aylesbury Manor was among the many properties owned by Anne's father, Thomas. Local legend says that Henry VIII visited the King's Head in the town when he was wooing Anne Boleyn.

6. Euclid Neale, who opened a clock-making workshop in Aylesbury in 1764, was regarded in the 18th century as one of the best clock makers in the country.

7. When first built, it was thought the sun reflecting off its large mirrored surface might prove to be a potential hazard to passing motorists, who could be blinded by its dazzle. To prevent this, a line of trees was planted alongside the main road to shield the glare.

8. In 1715 the then-owner of Chequers married John Russell, who was a grandson of Oliver Cromwell. The house still contains a large collection of Cromwell memorabilia.

9. The Cubitt Car, a 1922 Model K Tourer, which can be seen in the Buckinghamshire County Museum in Aylesbury. This car was made by the local Aylesbury firm Cubitt, and is one of only five Cubitt cars which are known to have survived. It was found in Australia in 1974, and brought back to England. It has now been restored and is a prized exhibit in its hometown museum.

10. Between 1809 and 1814, Hartwell House was leased to the exiled King of France, Louis XVIII. The arrival of the impoverished king and his court at Hartwell was not a happy experience for the mansion, as the once grand and imperious courtiers were reduced to farming chickens and other small livestock on its roof. King Louis signed the document which restored him to the French throne in the library of Hartwell House.

THE CANAL 1897 39642

WALTON POND c1950 A84002

FRANCIS FRITH

PIONEER VICTORIAN PHOTOGRAPHER

Francis Frith, founder of the world-famous photographic archive, was a complex and multi-talented man. A devout Quaker and a highly successful Victorian businessman, he was philosophical by nature and pioneering in outlook. By 1855 he had already established a wholesale grocery business in Liverpool, and sold it for the astonishing sum of £200,000, which is the equivalent today of over £15,000,000. Now in his thirties, and captivated by the new science of photography, Frith set out on a series of pioneering journeys up the Nile and to the Near East.

INTRIGUE AND EXPLORATION

He was the first photographer to venture beyond the sixth cataract of the Nile. Africa was still the mysterious 'Dark Continent', and Stanley and Livingstone's historic meeting was a decade into the future. The conditions for picture taking confound belief. He laboured for hours in his wicker dark-room in the sweltering heat of the desert, while the volatile chemicals fizzed dangerously in their trays. Back in London he exhibited his photographs and was 'rapturously cheered' by members of the Royal Society. His reputation as a photographer was made overnight.

VENTURE OF A LIFE-TIME

By the 1870s the railways had threaded their way across the country, and Bank Holidays and half-day Saturdays had been made obligatory by Act of Parliament. All of a sudden the working man and his family were able to enjoy days out, take holidays, and see a little more of the world.

With typical business acumen, Francis Frith foresaw that these new tourists would enjoy having souvenirs to commemorate their days out. For the next thirty years he travelled the country by train and by pony and trap, producing fine photographs of seaside resorts and beauty spots that were keenly bought by millions of Victorians. These prints were painstakingly pasted into family albums and pored over during the dark nights of winter, rekindling precious memories of summer excursions. Frith's studio was soon supplying retail shops all over the country, and by 1890 F Frith & Co had become the greatest specialist photographic publishing company in the world, with over 2,000 sales outlets, and pioneered the picture postcard.

FRANCIS FRITH'S LEGACY

Francis Frith had died in 1898 at his villa in Cannes, his great project still growing. By 1970 the archive he created contained over a third of a million pictures showing 7,000 British towns and villages.

Frith's legacy to us today is of immense significance and value, for the magnificent archive of evocative photographs he created provides a unique record of change in the cities, towns and villages throughout Britain over a century and more. Frith and his fellow studio photographers revisited locations many times down the years to update their views, compiling for us an enthralling and colourful pageant of British life and character.

We are fortunate that Frith was dedicated to recording the minutiae of everyday life. For it is this sheer wealth of visual data, the painstaking chronicle of changes in dress, transport, street layouts, buildings, housing and landscape that captivates us so much today, offering us a powerful link with the past and with the lives of our ancestors.

Computers have now made it possible for Frith's many thousands of images to be accessed almost instantly. The archive offers every one of us an opportunity to examine the places where we and our families have lived and worked down the years. Its images, depicting our shared past, are now bringing pleasure and enlightenment to millions around the world a century and more after his death.

For further information visit: www.francisfrith.com

INTERIOR DECORATION

Frith's photographs can be seen framed and as giant wall murals in thousands of pubs, restaurants, hotels, banks, retail stores and other public buildings throughout Britain. These provide interesting and attractive décor, generating strong local interest and acting as a powerful reminder of gentler days in our increasingly busy and frenetic world.

FRITH PRODUCTS

All Frith photographs are available as prints and posters in a variety of different sizes and styles. In the UK we also offer a range of other gift and stationery products illustrated with Frith photographs, although many of these are not available for delivery outside the UK – see our web site for more information on the products available for delivery in your country.

THE INTERNET

Over 100,000 photographs of Britain can be viewed and purchased on the Frith web site. The web site also includes memories and reminiscences contributed by our customers, who have personal knowledge of localities and of the people and properties depicted in Frith photographs. If you wish to learn more about a specific town or village you may find these reminiscences fascinating to browse. Why not add your own comments if you think they would be of interest to others? See **www.francisfrith.com**

PLEASE HELP US BRING FRITH'S PHOTOGRAPHS TO LIFE

Our authors do their best to recount the history of the places they write about. They give insights into how particular towns and villages developed, they describe the architecture of streets and buildings, and they discuss the lives of famous people who lived there. But however knowledgeable our authors are, the story they tell is necessarily incomplete.

Frith's photographs are so much more than plain historical documents. They are living proofs of the flow of human life down the generations. They show real people at real moments in history; and each of those people is the son or daughter of someone, the brother or sister, aunt or uncle, grandfather or grandmother of someone else. All of them lived, worked and played in the streets depicted in Frith's photographs.

We would be grateful if you would give us your insights into the places shown in our photographs: the streets and buildings, the shops, businesses and industries. Post your memories of life in those streets on the Frith website: what it was like growing up there, who ran the local shop and what shopping was like years ago; if your workplace is shown tell us about your working day and what the building is used for now. Read other visitors' memories and reconnect with your shared local history and heritage. With your help more and more Frith photographs can be brought to life, and vital memories preserved for posterity, and for the benefit of historians in the future.

Wherever possible, we will try to include some of your comments in future editions of our books. Moreover, if you spot errors in dates, titles or other facts, please let us know, because our archive records are not always completely accurate—they rely on 140 years of human endeavour and hand-compiled records. You can email us using the contact form on the website.

Thank you!

For further information, trade, or author enquiries please contact us at the address below:

The Francis Frith Collection, Frith's Barn, Teffont, Salisbury, Wiltshire, England SP3 5QP.

Tel: +44 (0)1722 716 376 Fax: +44 (0)1722 716 881

e-mail: sales@francisfrith.co.uk **www.francisfrith.com**